Everything
a child
should know about God

Everything a child should know about God

In easy words and pictures

Kenneth N. Taylor

CANDLE
BOOKS

First published in the UK by
Candle Books Ltd. 1998.
Distributed by STL., P.O. Box 300,
Carlisle, Cumbria CA3 0JH.

ISBN 1-85985-184-3

Illustrations copyright © 1995 by Bill Duca

Enquiries to:
Angus Hudson Ltd
Concorde House
Grenville Place
Mill Hill
London NW7 3SA
Tel +44 181 959 3668
Fax +44 181 959 3678

Printed in Hong Kong / China

Contents

PART 4
The Problem of Sin

PART 5
Jesus Comes to Help Us

PART 6
Jesus Wants to Save You

PART 7
The Holy Spirit Helps Us

PART 8
Why We Go to Church

A Note to Parents

The purpose of this colourful book is to teach young children about God. I believe that knowing God is the beginning of all wisdom. And I believe that children who are taught about God in their early years will be influenced for life in a very positive way.

I have been thinking about writing this book for a long time, and I believe it is one of the most important writings God has allowed me to do. Children learn with ease what they are taught early, whether from TV violence and pornography, or from life-changing biblical information, such as this book gives. It goes much beyond Bible story books, which are also so necessary.

This is a primer to tell children about God's eternity, and about Jesus Christ in heaven with His Father and why He came to earth to die. It tells of His going back to God in heaven and His coming again. The major Bible teachings about God are taught here, though so briefly and simply.

P.S. *This book is intended to be read to the child by Father or Mother.*

Part 1

All about the Bible

The Bible Tells Us about God

Here is a picture of the Bible. It is the best book in all the world. It tells us about God, who is the most important person in all the world.

QUESTION:
Whom does the Bible tell us about?

We Read the Bible to Learn about God

This is a picture of a family reading the Bible together. They do this every night. They are reading about God, our heavenly Father.

QUESTION:
Who is this family reading about?

Reading the Bible
Is Important

This boy's name is Kyle Johnson.
He is six years old, and he can
already read. He reads a little bit
from his Bible every day.
Sometimes he reads a story from
the Bible to his little sister Janice
because she is only four years old
and can't read yet. Reading the
Bible is very important.

QUESTIONS:
*How often does Kyle read from the
Bible? If you can't read yet, who can read
the Bible or a Bible story book to you?*

Prophets Wrote the Bible

This is a prophet. He lived a long time ago. He listened to God and wrote down what God said. He was writing part of the Bible. The Bible was written by many different people. God chose prophets, kings, and friends of Jesus to write down all the things He wanted us to know about Him.

QUESTION:
What is the prophet doing?

Jesus' Friends Wrote Parts of the Bible

God told many people to write parts of the Bible. One of the men God used for this was Paul, the apostle. God explained to Paul that Jesus died so we could be forgiven and be God's friends. Then Paul wrote it all down so we could read in the Bible the wonderful things God does for us. Here is a picture of Paul writing a letter to tell his friends about God. This letter became part of the Bible.

QUESTION:
What is the name of one of God's friends who wrote part of the Bible?

10

The Bible Is God's Special Book

No one but God knows what is going to happen to the world many years from now. Only He knows how to get to heaven when we die. He tells us His wonderful secrets in the book He has given to us. The name of His book is the Bible. It is the most wonderful book in the world because God Himself gave it to us.

QUESTION:
Why is the Bible the most wonderful book in the world?

Part 2

What God Has Done

God Made the World

The Bible tells us about God. He made our world and the sun and moon. He made billions of stars, too, and put them in the sky. We can see some of the worlds He made when we look up into the sky at night.

QUESTION:
Who made the world and the sun and stars?

God Made Plants and Animals

God made our beautiful world and all the trees and flowers. He made all the animals, too. Can you see the lion in the picture? Can you see the giraffe?

QUESTION:
Who made the animals and flowers?

God Made Angels

God made millions of angels, too. Usually we can't see them, but some people in the Bible saw an angel and talked to him. Some angels might be here in the room now! Angels are our helpers.

QUESTION:
Could there be any angels here in this room now?

God Made the First Man and Woman

Here is a picture of the very first man and the very first woman. Their names were Adam and Eve. God made Adam out of the ground and then made him become alive. Then God made Eve from part of Adam's side.

QUESTION:
What were the names of the first man and the first woman?

God Watches over the World

After God had created the plants, animals, Adam and Eve, and everything else in the world, He was very happy. God likes His creation. And He always cares about what happens to it. The Bible tells us that God cares about little birds as well as big kids like you! Thank you, God, for loving me and helping me.

QUESTION:
Finish this sentence with your name:
God loves and cares about

_____
(your first name)

_____.
(your last name)

24

Part 3

Who
God Is

God Has Always Lived

Where did God come from? Did
He have a father and mother? No,
God did not need a father and
mother. He has always been alive.
Who made God? No one did. God
has always been alive and is always
going to be alive.

QUESTION:
Did God have a father and mother?

God Is Spirit

God is a spirit. This means that
God is a person without a body.
You and I have bodies, but God
does not need a body. The girl in
the picture is showing how strong
her body is. God is there watching
her, but you can't see Him because
He doesn't have a body.

QUESTION:
Does God have a body?

God Is Loving

The Bible tells us that God loves
us. He likes to help us. He is our
Friend. He likes us to talk to Him.
We talk to Him when we pray.
The boy in the picture is talking
to God.

QUESTION:
How can you talk to God?

God Is Holy

God is holy. This means that He never does anything wrong. He always does what is right. No one else is holy like God, for all of us have sinned. God is perfect. He does not make mistakes or do bad things like the boy in the picture is doing.

QUESTION:
Who is holy and has never done anything wrong?

God Is Kind

Can you think of someone who is
very kind and nice to you? Perhaps
you think right away about your
father or mother, and that is good.
And there is Someone else who
likes to do nice things for us. I am
talking about God. He is kind to us
and forgives us.

QUESTION:
Who is someone who is kinder to you
than even your father or mother?

God Knows Everything

Carrie's mother is explaining to her that God knows what she is going to do next week—and next year. "God knows your name and where you live. He knows what everyone in the world is doing. He knows everything!"

QUESTIONS:
Do you know what you will do next year? Who knows this?

God Is Everywhere

"Is God up in heaven?" Bill asked his father. "Yes," his father told him, "and He is here with us in this room. And He is with Uncle Jim in the faraway country of Japan. God is everywhere at the same time!"

QUESTIONS:
Is God in heaven? Is He here in this room? Think of somewhere else He is right now.

40

God Is the Most Powerful Person in the World

Who is the strongest person you know? Even the strongest man on TV is not as strong as God. God is more powerful than anything on earth. That's because He made the world and everything in it. No one is more powerful than God.

QUESTION:
Is there anyone who is more powerful than God?

God Is One

Pastor Smith is visiting the primary class in Sunday school. He asked the children, "How many gods are there?" All the children told him, "There is only one God." "That is right," Pastor Smith said. "Some people think there are many gods, but there is only one."

QUESTION:
How many gods are there?

God Is Father, Son, and Holy Spirit

Pastor Smith told the children, "Our Father in heaven is God, and Jesus is God, and the Holy Spirit is God. But there is only one God. This is because God the Father, and Jesus, and the Holy Spirit are all parts of each other, and together they are only one God."

QUESTION:
How many Gods are there?

Part 4

The Problem of Sin

The Garden of Eden

After God created Adam and Eve, He put them in the Garden of Eden. It was a very beautiful place, and they were very happy.

QUESTION:
Where did God put Adam and Eve?

God Warns Adam and Eve

God told Adam and Eve that they could eat fruit from any of the trees in the Garden of Eden except the tree in the middle of the Garden. He said He would have to punish them if they disobeyed and ate fruit from that tree.

QUESTIONS:
What did God tell Adam and Eve not to do? What did God say He would do if they ate fruit from that tree?

Satan Tempts Adam and Eve

Some angels are good, and some angels are bad. The bad angels are called demons. Satan is in charge of all the bad angels. He turned himself into a beautiful snake and told Adam and Eve to disobey God. He told them to eat the fruit from the tree in the middle of the Garden, even though God said not to. Oh, I hope Adam and Eve don't listen to Satan! I hope they don't do what God said they must not do!

QUESTION:
What did Satan tell Adam and Eve to do?

Adam and Eve
Disobey God

I am sorry to say that Eve listened
to Satan and ate some of the fruit
and gave some to Adam, and he
ate it, too. They disobeyed God. To
disobey God is very bad. It is sin.

QUESTION:
What did Adam and Eve do?

God Punishes Adam and Eve

Adam and Eve were not happy anymore because they had disobeyed God. He had to punish them. He sent an angel to make them leave the beautiful garden. God told Adam and Eve that because they had disobeyed Him, they would have sadness and pain. That day they began to grow old and die.

QUESTIONS:
How did God punish Adam and Eve?
Why did He punish them?

We Are All Sinners

All of Adam and Eve's children and grandchildren and everyone else did bad things, too. How many bad things can you see happening in this picture? Why are they doing these things? It is because all of us have sin in our hearts. But God sent His Son, Jesus, to help us.

QUESTION:
Do you ever do things you shouldn't? God sent Jesus so that you can be forgiven for your sins.

Part 5

Jesus Comes to Help Us

Jesus Is God's Son

The Bible tells us about Jesus. He is God's Son. God loves Him very much. And God loves you, too. God loved you so much that He sent His Son, Jesus, from heaven to help you by dying for your sins. Now God can forgive you for the wrong things you do.

QUESTION:
What is the name of God's Son?

Jesus Has Always Lived

This is Jesus when He lived on earth. The Bible tells us He lived in heaven before He came to earth. He had lived in heaven with God, His Father, forever and ever. Then He came to earth to help us.

QUESTION:
Where did Jesus live before He came to earth?

Jesus Leaves His Home in Heaven

Jesus is God's Son. He lived with His Father up in heaven. He looked down at the world and saw the people doing bad things. He knew God must punish them. But God didn't want to punish the people who did bad things. So Jesus and His Father agreed on a special plan. Jesus said, "I will go down to earth, and you must punish me instead of the people who sin. They deserve to die, but I will die instead." In the picture Sara's mum is pointing to heaven, where Jesus lived before He came to earth.

QUESTION:
Why did Jesus leave His home in heaven and live down here on earth?

Jesus Becomes a Baby

So Jesus left His wonderful home in heaven and came down here to earth to help us. Did He come to earth as an angel? No, He came as a baby! Did He come as a mighty king? No, but as a baby! That way, He didn't scare anybody. Would you be afraid of a baby? Of course not!

QUESTION:
Did Jesus come to earth as a powerful king?

An Angel Talks to Mary

Here is a picture of the angel Gabriel telling Mary that she would have a baby. Gabriel said the baby would be the Son of God and that His name would be Jesus.

QUESTION:
What did the angel tell Mary?

Jesus Is Born

Mary and her husband, Joseph, were on a trip when the baby was ready to be born. They couldn't find a place to stay, so they stayed in a barn. That night Jesus, God's Son, was born there where the cows, sheep, and donkeys lived. How strange that the one who made the world would be born in a barn, and not in a beautiful house!

QUESTIONS:
Was Jesus born in a beautiful house?
Where was Jesus born?

An Angel Talks
to the Shepherds

On the night when Jesus was born, some shepherds were out in the fields taking care of their sheep. Suddenly an angel appeared and told them, "Jesus, God's Son, is born in the town of Bethlehem."

QUESTIONS:
What did the angel tell the shepherds?
Who was born that night in Bethlehem?

Angels Praise God

Then the sky was filled with angels shouting, "Glory to God." They were happy because God's Son had come to earth to help us.

QUESTION:
Why were the angels happy?

Shepherds Worship Jesus

The shepherds ran to the little town of Bethlehem, where the baby Jesus was born. They got down on their knees and worshipped Him because He is the Son of God.

QUESTION:
Why did the shepherds get down on their knees in front of the baby?

Wise Men Visit Jesus

Later, some wise men came from far away and brought presents for Jesus. Do you know why? It is because Jesus is God's Son. He is a mighty king.

QUESTIONS:
Can you see the wise men in the picture? What are they giving to God's Son?

The Boy Jesus
Teaches Grown-Ups

Here is a picture of Jesus when He was 12 years old. He is telling these men about God. Jesus knew about God because He had always been with God in heaven before He was born.

QUESTION:
How did Jesus know all about God?

Jesus Chooses 12 Helpers

When Jesus grew up, He chose 12 young men to be His special friends. They are called disciples. They went with Him wherever He went, and Jesus taught them about God.

QUESTIONS:
What were Jesus' 12 special friends called? Can you count the disciples in the picture?

Jesus Heals a Blind Man

Jesus did many wonderful things like making sick people well. Here He is making a blind man see. He told the blindness to go away, and right away the man could see.

QUESTION:
How long did it take Jesus to make the blind man see?

Jesus Brings a
Girl Back to Life

Here Jesus is making a girl who
was dead come back to life again!
What wonderful things Jesus did.
He could do these things because
He is God's Son.

QUESTION:
*What happened to the girl who was
dead?*

Jesus Does Miracles

In this picture you can see Jesus walking on the water. Can you walk on top of the water? Of course not! But Jesus could because He is God's Son.

QUESTIONS:
What is Jesus doing? Why could He do this?

Long Live the King!

Many people wanted Jesus to be their king. In this picture, they are waving palms and putting their coats along the road in front of the donkey that Jesus is riding on. They did this to show Him that they knew He was great and good.

QUESTION:
What are the people doing?

Some People Hated Jesus

But some people didn't want Jesus to be the king. They were angry and jealous of Him. They sent soldiers to capture Jesus and take Him to jail.

QUESTION:
What are the soldiers doing?

Pilate Lets the People Kill Jesus

Then Jesus' enemies took Jesus to a man named Pilate. He decided what to do with Jesus. He let them have Jesus, and they took Him away to kill Him. You can see Him carrying the cross He will die on.

QUESTION:
What is Jesus carrying?

Jesus Dies on a Cross

The soldiers nailed Jesus' hands and feet to the cross and left Him there to die. Had He been bad? Is that why He was being killed? No, He had never done anything wrong. He was dying for your sins and mine. God was punishing Him for the bad things we have done. He died in our place. Now God can forgive us for being bad if we ask Him to.

QUESTIONS:
Who died for your sins? Do you want to ask Him to forgive you and to be your Saviour and Lord? Let's do it now. You can pray, "Thank you, Jesus, for dying for my sins."

Jesus Dies for Our Sins

Was Jesus dying because He was bad? No, He was good. In all His life He had never done anything bad. God punished Him for the bad things that Adam and Eve did, and that you and I have done. This was the special plan Jesus and His Father agreed on. How kind of Jesus to do this for us! How much He loves us! How thankful we can be!

QUESTION:
Why should we thank Jesus?

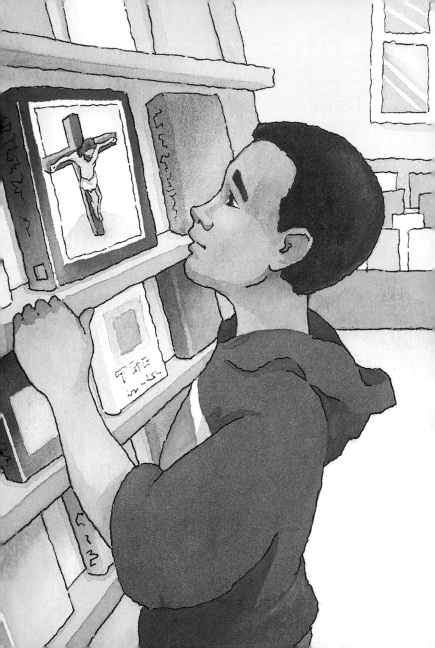

Jesus' Friends Are Sad

Kind friends are taking Jesus' body down from the cross. They are very sad. They thought Jesus would be a mighty king, but instead, now He has been killed, and He is dead.

QUESTION:
Why are Jesus' friends sad?

Jesus Is Buried

Jesus' friends have put Jesus' dead body in this cave and are rolling a big stone in front of it to keep out dogs and other animals.

QUESTION:
Why are they rolling the big stone?

Mary Meets an Angel

Early on Sunday morning, three days after Jesus died, suddenly there was a great earthquake. An angel of the Lord came down from heaven, rolled aside the stone, and sat on it. His face shone like lightning, and his clothing was a brilliant white. When Mary went out to the cave, the angel told her, "Jesus isn't here! He is alive again!" God had made Jesus alive again!

QUESTION:
How did the cave get empty?

Jesus' Friends Look for His Body

Peter and John, who were close friends of Jesus, heard that His grave was empty. They ran out to see. And sure enough, the stone in front of the entrance was rolled back. They went into the cave and saw where Jesus' dead body had been lying, but Jesus wasn't there. God had raised Him from the dead!

QUESTIONS:
Did Peter and John see Jesus' body lying in the cave? Why not?

110

Jesus Is Alive!

Three days after Jesus was killed, God made Him alive again. He isn't dead anymore! We celebrate this wonderful event each year at Easter time. It is called the Resurrection. God raised Jesus from death. In the picture it is Easter Day, and God's people at church are singing about God raising Jesus from the dead. He is alive!

QUESTION:
What did God do for Jesus?

Jesus Visits His Friends

Later on the same day that Jesus became alive again, Jesus' friends were in a room together. Suddenly Jesus was standing there talking to them! He didn't open the door and come in because it was locked. He must have come through the wall! He could do things like that because Jesus is God.

QUESTION:
How did Jesus get into the room?

Jesus Goes Back to Heaven

Several weeks later, Jesus and His friends were standing on a hill. Suddenly He began rising into the sky and disappeared into a cloud! He went back to His Father in heaven, where He had always been before He became a baby here on earth.

QUESTIONS:
Where did Jesus go? Had He been in heaven before? When?

116

Jesus Will Come Back

Suddenly two angels appeared among Jesus' friends and told them, "Jesus will come back again someday. He will come in the clouds, just the way He left." When Jesus comes back, He will take His friends to heaven to be with Him forever. He might come back today. Are you one of His friends?

QUESTION:
Is Jesus going to return from heaven?

Jesus Prays for Us

While Jesus is away in heaven, He prays for us and talks to God His Father about us. He tells God we are His friends and asks Him to forgive our sins and help us. What a friend we have in Jesus! In the picture you can see Jesus with two of His friends. You can be His friend, too.

QUESTION:
What is Jesus doing now?

Jesus Loves You

Did Jesus die for you? Yes! Does Jesus love you? Yes! Jesus said, "Let the little children come to Me." The Bible says, "Believe on the Lord Jesus Christ and you will be saved."

QUESTION:
Do you know this little song? Let's say it or sing it together:

"Jesus loves me! this I know,
For the Bible tells me so."

Part 6

Jesus Wants to Save You

We Are All Sinners

Every one of us has done things
that are bad. God said not to, but
we did them anyway. Have you
ever told a lie? That was a sin. Have
you ever taken something that
didn't belong to you? That was a
sin.

QUESTION:
Have you ever sinned?

Jesus Wants to Save You

Jesus died for you because he wanted to be your Saviour. He will be glad to forgive your sins if you ask Him to. He wants you to come and talk to Him about it. You can tell Him, "Thank You for dying for me. Come into my heart, Lord Jesus." Do you want to do that now?

QUESTION:
What should you tell Jesus?

Jesus Takes Away Our Sins

God always punishes sin. So will God punish us because we have done bad things? No, for Jesus Christ our Lord gave Himself to be punished instead of us. He died on the cross because of our sins. Now God can forgive us and look at us as if we had never sinned! Thank You, Jesus, for taking away our sins!

QUESTION:
Who was punished by God because of your sins?

You Are Part of God's Family

When you become a Christian, you become part of God's family. He wants to love you as His own son or daughter. He wants to help your mum and dad take care of you. He will tell you when you do something wrong, and He is happy when you do what is right. God wants you to know that you are very special to Him. In the picture John is painting his family. I hope they all know about Jesus.

QUESTION:
Tell the names of some people God loves. Did you say your name, too?

We Can Live with Jesus in Heaven

God has always been alive and is always going to be alive. You will always be alive, too. Someday our bodies will grow old and die. Then, if we love Jesus, we can go and live with God in heaven. The Bible tells us that heaven is a beautiful place and everyone is very happy there. Heaven will be a wonderful place to live! This girl is thinking about how wonderful heaven is.

QUESTION:
If you love Jesus, what beautiful place can you go to after you die?

134

Thank You, Jesus!

We need to thank Jesus because of all of His kindness. In this picture, Ashley is praying with her mother. Would you like to pray, too? Let's do it now. "Thank You, Jesus, for dying for my sins. I'm happy that I will be able to live with You in heaven someday. Thank You for making me part of Your family! Amen."

QUESTION:
Who died so that your sins can be forgiven?

136

Part 7

The Holy Spirit Helps Us

The Holy Spirit Is God

Here is something wonderful to remember: Our heavenly Father is God, and Jesus is God, and the Holy Spirit is God. And yet there is only one God because they are all parts of each other. Now we are going to talk about God the Holy Spirit. He lives in heaven and here on earth, and He lives within His people. He gives us power and fills us with joy. The people in this picture are God's friends. They have the Holy Spirit within them, and they are happy and friendly.

QUESTION:
Who is our special Friend and Helper?

The Holy Spirit Helps Us

Let me tell you something that is very wonderful about the Holy Spirit. He helps us to be good. He can help us to be kind and gentle. He helps us not to be mean to other kids. He helps us to obey our parents and do it right away. He will help us at school, too. He is helping the boy in this picture to be kind. The Holy Spirit always wants to help us. Just pray and ask Him to help you!

QUESTION:
Who can help you to be kind and obedient?

142

The Holy Spirit Comes to Jesus' Friends

A few days after Jesus went back to heaven, His friends were together in a room where they were praying. Suddenly, there was a roaring noise. Flames of fire came on the head of each of them, but the fire didn't burn them or hurt them. This was the Holy Spirit, whom Jesus sent to help them.

QUESTION:
Tell what happened after there was a roaring noise.

The Holy Spirit Helps Jesus' Friends Preach

After the tongues of fire came on the heads of Jesus' friends, they went outside and began preaching in languages they had never learned! Everyone was very surprised that they could talk in these other languages. They could do this because God's Holy Spirit helped them.

QUESTION:
How were Jesus' friends able to speak in languages they hadn't learned?

Jesus' Friends Do Miracles

The Holy Spirit gave power to some of Jesus' friends to make sick people well and to make dead people live again. In this picture you can see Jesus' friends healing the sick.

QUESTION:
What power did the Holy Spirit give to some of Jesus' friends?

Jesus' Friends Tell Others

Jesus' friends liked to tell other people about Jesus. But sometimes the people they talked to got angry. They didn't love God. They hurt Jesus' friends and told them not to talk about Jesus anymore. In this picture, Paul is telling the people about Jesus. Some people are very angry and are going to throw big rocks at him, but Paul is not afraid. He would rather be hurt or killed than stop telling others about how wonderful Jesus is. The Holy Spirit helped him to be brave.

QUESTION:
Will Paul stop talking about Jesus even if people throw rocks at him?

Part 8

Why We Go to Church

How the Church Began

In the last picture we saw a man being hurt because he loved Jesus. Many of Jesus' friends had to move to other towns and countries to be safe. These Christians told their new neighbours and friends about Jesus. They met together to sing to Jesus and give thanks to God. They encouraged and helped each other. When they came together this way they were a church. That is how many churches started in many new countries.

QUESTION:
What did Jesus' friends talk to their neighbours about?

What Is the Church?

Most people who believe in Jesus meet together every week. They read the Bible, sing songs, pray, and encourage one another. That's why we go to church. Church is a great place to worship God and make new friends! In the picture you can see people going to church.

QUESTION:
What do people do in church?

We Go to Church to Learn about God

These children are at church. They will meet lots of other children there and sing praise and give thanks to God. If they didn't go to church each week, they would gradually forget about how wonderful God is. I am glad they are going to church, aren't you?

QUESTION:
Why is it good to go to Sunday school and church every week?

We Go to Church to Be Baptised

When Jesus was on earth, He was baptised by His friend John. Jesus tells us that we should be baptised, too. Baptism tells others that you belong to Jesus. Baptism is very special. Ask your mum or dad to tell you about baptism in your church. In the picture John is baptising Jesus.

QUESTION:
What is happening to Jesus?

We Go to Church for the Lord's Supper

On the night before Jesus died on the cross, He ate His last supper with His twelve disciples. He wanted to do something special to help them remember Him. So Jesus took some bread, thanked God for it, and gave it to the disciples. He also took a cup, thanked God, and told His friends to drink from the cup. In the picture you can see Jesus giving his disciples the bread. When we do this in church, it reminds us that Jesus died for our sins and that we are God's friends.

QUESTION:
What does Jesus want us to remember?

Part 9

Living as Jesus' Friends

Jesus' Friends Are Kind

Here are two children who love Jesus. They are picking flowers to take to a neighbour who is sick. They are being kind. The Holy Spirit inside them is helping them to be kind.

QUESTION:
Who is helping the children to be kind?

Jesus' Friends Pray

Here is Carl Jennings. He is talking to God, his heavenly Father. God likes it when Carl comes and talks to Him. You can talk to God, too—perhaps just before you go to bed. We can talk to God anytime. We don't need to be on our knees.

QUESTION:
When can we talk to God?

Jesus' Friends Tell Others

God wants His people to tell others what Jesus has done for them. Here are three ways you can help:

1. Tell your friends about Jesus.
2. Bring them to Sunday school so the teacher can help you tell them.
3. Give some of your money to the church so the church can send it to missionaries. They tell people in other countries about Jesus. In the picture Timothy is telling his friend about Jesus.

QUESTION:
What can you do to help other children learn about Jesus?

Jesus' Friends
Are Thankful

Sometimes in church we sing:

"Praise God from whom all
    blessings flow.
Praise Him, all creatures here below.
Praise Him above, you heavenly host.
Praise Father, Son, and Holy Ghost!"

We should praise God and thank
Him every day. Let's pray this
prayer together now: "Thank You,
God, for loving us. We praise You
because You are so wonderful."

QUESTION:
Why should we praise God?

Part 10

When Jesus Comes Back

Jesus Will Come Back

Jesus is in heaven now, but someday He will come back again through the clouds. We will see Him. And He will take us to heaven to live with Him. What an exciting day that will be! Perhaps He will come today! In the picture this family is talking about what it will be like to see Jesus come back from heaven.

QUESTION:
Who is going to come back again from heaven?

God Will Punish the Wicked

Someday God will punish everyone who deserves it, except those whose sins have been forgiven. Jesus says for us to come to Him and He will save us.

QUESTION:
What happens when we come to Jesus?

God Will Bring Peace

When Jesus comes back, God will give us peace on earth, with no more killing and crying. Everyone will obey Him and do what is right. How wonderful that will be! The Bible tells us to pray, "Come soon, Lord Jesus."

QUESTION:
Why do we want the Lord Jesus to come soon?

Just
Remember...

God Is with You

God always knows what is the best thing for you to do. He is always glad to help you know what He wants you to do. You are His child, and He will be with you and help you today and tomorrow and every day for all of your life.

QUESTION:
Who wants to help you every day of your life?

The Ten Commandments

In the Bible God tells us about His love
for us and tells us what He wants us to do.
He also tells us other things He wants us
never to do. In the next few pages of this
book, I will tell you some of His good
rules.

1. YOU MUST NOT WORSHIP
   OTHER GODS.
This means we must never worship
anyone but God. We must love Him with
all of our hearts, praying to Him who is
our only God.

2. DO NOT MAKE AN IDOL.
In some countries, people make statues
and worship them as if they were God.
God tells us not to do this.

3. DO NOT MISUSE
   THE NAME OF GOD.
It is wrong to use His name carelessly or
angrily, but we should use His name to
talk to Him in prayer and to praise Him
and thank Him.

4. REMEMBER THE SABBATH DAY TO KEEP IT HOLY.

We are to show that we love God by going to church every week. In this way we hear the Bible read and explained to us. It is good for us to be with others who love God.

5. HONOUR YOUR FATHER AND YOUR MOTHER.

We are to love our parents and to treat them with respect and honour. For instance, we are not to talk back to them. We are to do what they tell us to do and not do what they tell us we shouldn't do.

6. YOU SHALL NOT KILL.

This commandment from God means that it is wrong to murder people. God has given them their lives to use for Him, and we must not carelessly take their lives away from them. God says not to hurt or harm other people but to help them.

7. HUSBANDS AND WIVES

God gives husbands to their wives, and

He gives wives to their husbands. God does not want them ever to leave each other and marry someone else. Instead, they are to love and protect each other always, and help each other. God will help them, and if they have children, He will help the children, too.

8. YOU MUST NOT STEAL.
God says that we may not take money or other things that don't belong to us. We must not sneak away with what belongs to someone else, no matter how much we want it.

9. YOU MUST NOT TELL LIES.
God wants us to be honest and truthful all the time. If you have an accident and break something, like a dish, say that you did it and are sorry. Don't lie about it or say that someone else broke the dish. That would be wrong, and God does not want you to tell lies.

10. YOU MUST NOT WANT WHAT ISN'T YOURS.

Perhaps someone has a toy that you wish you had. You must wait until you can earn enough money to buy it, or perhaps you might get it for Christmas or a birthday present. But God does not want you thinking or worrying about it and feeling sorry for yourself because you don't have it now. Instead, you are to be happy with what God has given you—your parents and your home and so many other good things.

Doctrinal Index